THE GOLF STANDARD

PREPARE FOR BETTER GOLF

JEFF MITCHELL

The Golf Standard has videos available for a variety of topics, including course management, routines, game management and many others.

Go to: golfswing.com

CONTENTS

PART I
THE GOLF STANDARD

Foreword   3
Observations   5
What is The Golf Standard?   7
Chapter 1   9
Chapter 2   17
Chapter 3   21
Chapter 4   25
Chapter 5   29
Chapter 6   33

PART II
ROUTINE SUCCESS

Foreword   37
Chapter 1   39
Chapter 2   41
Chapter 3   45
Chapter 4   51
Chapter 5   57
Chapter 6   59
Chapter 7   61

PART III
GAME AND COURSE MANAGEMENT

Foreword   65
Chapter 1   67
Chapter 2   73
Chapter 3   77
Chapter 4   79
Chapter 5   83

Chapter 6   87

PART IV
TOURNAMENT PREPARATION
Foreword   91
Chapter 1   93
Chapter 2   95
Chapter 3   97
Chapter 4   99
Chapter 5   103
Chapter 6   107
Chapter 7   109
Chapter 8   113
Chapter 9   115
Chapter 10   117
Chapter 11   119

About the Author   121

PART I

THE GOLF STANDARD

FOREWORD

It is with a tremendous amount of pride and gratitude that I put this information together about the game of golf. I am blessed beyond measure and have been lucky in my life in every way that matters. I have played golf around the world and in almost every state in the US. I have played on the biggest stage, having played on the PGA Tour for 8 years and 2 years of Champion's Tour golf. And, even after having 13 top ten finishes, 27 top 25 finishes, and making 110 career cuts on the PGA Tour, I am still trying to figure out whether winning the 1980 Phoenix Open or leading after the first round of the 1980 Masters is my biggest thrill in the game. Accomplishment and the history of the game both have their place in my heart.

After leaving the tour, I started teaching and fell in love working with junior golfers. After a suggestion from my mother-in-law and a lot of support from my wife, I went back to college and then into coaching at Texas Tech University. I spent 10 years at Texas Tech, 4 years at Stanford University, and 7 years at the University of North Texas. Honestly, I am not sure who learned more from those years: the student/athletes or me. It was a tremendous experience and one I will draw on for the rest of my life.

With 10 years of PGA Tour/Champions Tour experience, teaching for 30 years and coaching for 21 years, my view of how the game is played and, more importantly, how it is taught has been completely transformed.

Over the past 50 years, the average golf handicap has hardly changed. PGA Tour players are shooting lower scores, but I wonder how much of that can be attributed to equipment, the amazing condition of golf courses, and being able to play around the world. No doubt, it is a different world out there for the elite players. The problem is that the elite player makes up less than 1% of 1% of golfers around the world. The question is, "how can the other 99.9% improve and enjoy the game?"

The Golf Standard is a comprehensive program designed to teach you how to play the game, not just swing a club. Don't get me wrong, you have to learn and understand basic fundamentals of the game. But, you don't have to have Tom Watson's imagination, or Bubba Watson's length. With some basic understanding of fundamentals and a plan, you can be a very competent and consistent player. I like to look at the competency aspect as *"Measure Up".* If you know what you want, you keep track of what you are actually doing, and you know where you want to go, you can get there.

I hope you enjoy your journey.

Jeff Mitchell
PGA Tour Life Member
PGA Life Member

OBSERVATIONS

"I went out Saturday and played 18 holes. The first 5 holes were just awful. I was rusty and just couldn't find a rhythm. I finally started putting it together from 6 until 14 and then it all fell apart again. I just can't get off to a good start and once I get it figured out, I can't finish it off."

"I make a few pars and a couple birdies in almost every round. If it weren't for the 2 doubles and a triple every round, I would be happy with my game,"

"Why does it seem like I am always in between clubs?"

"Every time my irons are clicking, my driver leaves me."

"Invariably if I am playing well tee to green, my short game is poor, or vice versa."

"I played in a tournament recently. I had some of the worst lies I have ever seen. Why does that always seem to happen when it matters the most?"

Ever hear the line, "To make a real and positive change in your game takes a LOT of time and repetitions, and your scores are going to suffer for a while." Not true. What it takes is belief in your method and commitment to your shots. With a consistent and proper routine, you can make that change without going backwards.

Have you ever wondered why it is so difficult to maintain consistency in your game even when you practice on a fairly regular basis?

Wouldn't it be nice if there were a way to, not only maintain a level of play, but also improve over a period of time, with only a modest amount of practice? You can probably stop searching. The answer might just be right in front of you.

Quality not quantity is an old but true saying. It is one of the principles of this book and it is one of the principles of success in most any endeavor.

If any of the prior statements sounds familiar, the information in this book will improve your golf.

WHAT IS THE GOLF STANDARD?

By means of comparison, the Golf Standard is similar to the Gold Standard. The Gold Standard is a unit of measure that other systems are valued by and/or compared to. For our purposes, that means:

> *Identifying, trusting and staying true to your STANDARD, and consistently integrating YOUR method into your practice, play and competition.*

For every golfer, there are elements in your game that are positive and are identifiable as strengths. The issue might just be your ability to identify those elements and strengths, and once identified, to exploit them.

Remember, "golf is not about perfection, it is about repetition". The key is finding *your* standard and integrating that standard into your game by a process of belief in your method and repetition.

By making a series of calculations about the strengths in your game, you can "MEASURE UP". To Measure Up means to take the guesswork out of the process and allow you to make continuous and consistent progress toward your goals.

Why the Golf Standard?

Once you understand your STANDARD, your METHOD, you can take it to the course and maximize your results. It isn't enough to learn how to swing a club. You have to be able to transfer that from the range to the course. **Realize your potential in your game.**

Jeff Mitchell
    PGA Tour Life Member
    PGA Life Member

CHAPTER 1

IDENTIFYING YOUR STANDARD

FULL SWING

Before we get started, I would like to ask you one question. It is a 50-50 question. It is also a trick question. To get it correct, you have to get the answer, plus have the correct explanation of why you are correct.

Here goes: Which is more important in golf - direction or distance? Think about it before you answer. Remember, you have to have the correct reason for the answer, not just the answer. I also have to tell you, I have asked this question over 1000 times and only about 5 golfers have answered this correctly for the correct reason. The "trick" part of it is that you have to answer the question the way I would. The answer is at the end of this chapter.

SITUATION

The best players in the world can change the distance they hit a club by swinging easier or harder. They can also hook

and slice the ball, seemingly, at will. The reality is that 1% of
the top 1% are able to do that with any degree of consistency.
They, though, hit hundreds of balls a day, 300 days a year. For
those of you that don't have that time to spend, the goal is to
find and cultivate a simple, dependable and repeatable swing.
It is interesting how most golfers will completely change the
way they swing the club when the target is 5 yards away from
their optimal yardage. And, by doing so they will hit the ball
15-20 yards away from their target because the rhythm and
balance and feel will completely disappear.

PROCESS
   "Measure Up".
   I have never been a fan of having a "Favorite" club. But, if
you do have one, consider yourself lucky. It might be your
favorite because you happened to have hit some really good
shots with it, or, more importantly, it just might be the club
that fits your "full" swing. That club is your "STANDARD".
Having that "Standard" allows you to model other clubs by it.
For example: My so-called favorite club is a 9-iron. I feel like I
have the best combination of distance control and directional
control. With that in mind, I have created a golf bag full of 9-
irons. What if you could hit your favorite club on every shot,
on every course, every day! What if the yardage was always
perfect and you never felt like you were in between clubs!
Well, it is and you can! When I stand on the tee on a par 4 or a
par 5, I imagine that I have a 9-iron in my hands. I take my
normal 9-iron swing and get great results. This works with any
club at any target at any time, as long it is a "full" swing. Plus,
you can grip a club down ½ " and take 5-6 yards off the shot
simply because of physics. That ½" is equivalent to approxi-

mately 2 miles per hour of clubhead speed as long as you do not influence the swing in any other fashion. You never have to be *in between* clubs again. If being 15 feet away from your target is too far you need to either turn pro ..... or take up bowling.

To test this "9-iron" theory, go to the range. After warming up, take out your favorite club and hit two full shots. Then change to any other club in your bag. Hit two full shots with that other club. Regardless of the outcome, immediately hit 2 more full shots with your favorite club. Does the favorite club still feel the same? Did you still get great results with it? If the answer is yes, you are on a very positive track to a more consistent golf game. If the answer is no, it means you changed your swing with the other club and it shows up in the results of your favorite club. This 2-ball drill might be your nightmare short term. Psychologically, it is not easy. But if you stick with it, long term, it will become your salvation.

And by the way, golf clubs are not complicated. An 8 iron is 1/2" longer than a 9 iron and the 8 iron has 4 degrees less loft. The combination of the two create 10-13 yards difference in how far you hit them depending on the clubhead speed of your full swing. An 8 iron is also slightly lighter than a 9 iron. Clubs are designed this way so that when you pick them up they all "feel" like they are the same weight as the 9 iron. The cool thing about this is that it allows you to have ONE swing for all your clubs. Your ONE swing is unique to you and no one else. It is YOUR swing. The more you learn to take advantage of it, the more fun the game will become.

Which brings me to an interesting question: what is a "full" swing?

A full swing is the swing you take when you hit it as far as you can while maintaining great balance and making solid contact. I encourage you to find your full swing. Test your swing to find out just how much you can handle. In golf, the farther you can hit it, the easier courses become. This doesn't mean, though, that you are swinging as hard as you can. Your maximum and your full are two different swings. Chances are your full swing is going to be around 75-80% of your maximum. Understanding that distinction will help you with your shot control and help to avoid fatigue. If your game seems to suffer over the last few holes, it might be your muscles are getting tired but you are trying to get the same results out of your swing. This can have a detrimental affect on your swing and on your mental state. It is easy for frustration or panic to creep into your game. In football if you aren't getting the results you want you are probably not trying hard enough. In golf if you aren't getting the results you want, it could very well be that you are trying too hard.

The good news and the bad news about having identified and learned how to develop your STANDARD is that you now understand about 5% of the game.

Having identified YOUR standard, it is time to understand how to take advantage of that knowledge and attack that other 95%.

First and with your standard in mind you must identify the strengths of your game.

What is a strength? Strengths in your game are defined as any element that you can repeat on a consistent basis and that gives you the desired result.

EXAMPLES MIGHT BE:

  1. Good lag putting. This gives you the ability to aim

for the middle of greens or to a more conservative spot on the green when your approach shot is from a difficult angle or from a long distance away from the green.

2. Solid ball contact when chipping. This gives you options when choosing a club to chip with. I try to chip the ball as low as possible while landing it on the green and on a smooth level area of the green. But if you can count on solid contact you might be able to take a sand wedge and fly a ball over a slope of green and onto a plateau that has a relatively small target area to hit to. By doing that you can control the first bounce, and that is a big advantage.

3. Good distance control with a 50-75 yard pitch shot. This is a strength not only for laying back on a par 5 to set up a good approach, but so that if you hit a ball into the rough or in some trouble with your tee shot on a par 4, you can place your second to a yardage you are really good with and have a much better chance to save a par.

4. A consistent yardage gap between clubs. If your gap is 10-13 yards, but consistent, then you never have to be in between clubs. If the yardage is in the middle of two clubs, take the longer one, grip down ½ inch and no other adjustments need to be made. As long as you do not alter your swing, the ball will travel almost exactly ½ club shorter.

5. A high trajectory with your irons and woods. This gives you the ability to aim over obstacles and stop the ball quickly. Being able to aim directly over a bunker to keep a ball below the pin is a definite advantage.

6. A low trajectory with your irons or woods. This can also be a strength especially if you play in windy conditions or on courses with few forced carries. You can negate much of the wind and/or you can gain yardage on the ground with your carry and roll.

7. Stamina. This may sound odd, but being fit gives you the ability to count on the same result with a swing late in the round as you have early in the round.

8. You hit the ball far. The obvious advantage is that you can reach par 5 holes in two. You can also, though, hit a shorter iron into par 3's, and approach shots on par 4's. Shorter clubs tend to have more spin. That gives you more control in the air and on the ground. Even if you do hit the ball into trouble, it gives you more options for recovery, too.

9. Consistent pattern of shot. Regardless of whether you draw the ball or fade the ball, being able to count on the ball going one direction or the other lets you aim with that pattern in mind. It gives you a larger target area to play to. Jack Nicklaus hit a fade with a high percentage of his shots. When he had a shot into a green, he would aim 15 feet left of the flag. If he hit it straight, he was 15 feet away. If he faded the ball he would end up close to the hole. If he sliced it, he would end up 15 feet right of the hole. By being able to count on the ball curving one direction he gave himself the opportunity to hit a "marginal" shot and still get a good result. Nicklaus understood his tendencies.

LET'S ASSUME that you have gone through and identified 8-10 things that you feel like you do well. That is "game management". Obviously, as you practice you want to be able to add to that list by identifying other areas where you are not as proficient and make them strengths, too. But now it is time to use YOUR current strengths to your advantage. With those strengths in mind, let's identify ways to use your "course management" skills.

Architects are complicated in many respects and quite simple in others. Golf courses are designed with budgets, water, climate, and the anticipated clientele in mind. They are also designed with the personality of the designer in mind. For example, a golf course in Phoenix, Arizona is most likely going to have a relatively small amount of green grass areas and a large amount of native grasses and desert integrated into the design because of water availability. If it is a resort or private course, it might be somewhat different because of clientele and financial resources. This type of golf course is going to be very "target" oriented. You may have to play to more conservative targets because the penalties for missing the green grass are so severe. Also, these types of courses can be very visually intimidating. Chances are it will test your commitment to shot and your short game.

TRICK QUESTION ANSWER: Distance. Reason-There is no question that direction is hugely important to success in golf. But, to achieve directional control, you have to have a swing that is repeatable and with a consistent release point. Creating consistent distance with full shots requires that you use the same effort level and have a rhythmic swing. If you have a rhythmic swing and are consistent with the effort level, you will create a repeatable shot shape. By controlling the distance, you will have control over the direction. In reverse, the more you obsess over direction, the more your directional control will suffer. Simply put: repeatable distance control = directional control.

---

* IF YOU WANT to put this to the test, go to the range and hit 5 balls in a row with any club with a full swing. If your distance is consistent, you will find that the directional pattern is very consistent, also.

CHAPTER 2

PUTTING

SITUATION

Have you noticed that you putt well on a certain type and/or speed of green? Some people love fast greens and some love slow greens. There is probably a speed that fits you just right. That is your STANDARD. For many golfers, that is their home course. Unfortunately, all greens aren't that speed. But, if you can identify the speed that suits you best, you can easily learn to adjust to other greens. If done right, you can adjust to any green in 3 putts. That's right....3 putts! If learned, you will never have to change your "standard". All greens at that point will be the same as your "home course", or the course where you feel the most comfortable. Your comfortable course becomes your "home course". In other words, if 10 is the perfect speed for you, you just have to make *all* greens putt at 10.

You have to stay true to YOUR stroke-YOUR speed-YOUR STANDARD!

Process

"Measure Up".

Go to a golf course where you have had a lot of success putting. Ask the pro how fast the greens are running. He will most likely say 9 or 10 or 11 on the STIMPMETER*. If you are familiar with this terminology, that's great. If not, see the explanation at the end of the chapter.

Let's say the green is 10 on the STIMPMETER (10 is considered about medium speed). Now, place two quarters on the green exactly 15 feet apart and on a level part of the green. Practice putting from one quarter and back to the other, trying to stop the ball on top of the quarter. It is practically impossible to do so, but it gets you zoned in on the speed aspect of the green. Once you get a really good sense of 15 feet on a "10" speed green, spend some time working on putts of varying length on that green. Don't be concerned about the direction, just the speed. It is very rare that you will miss a putt by more than even a foot, direction wise. It is common that you will miss putts by 2 feet or more, distance wise. If, though, you are good at speed control on a "10", you can be good at any speed. If 10 is really your speed, you probably won't struggle much with putts at most any length. If you do struggle, pay close attention to the putts that you are not pleased with. Is there a common denominator to where they end up, either short or long. If there is, you might have to adjust "your" speed. If you are ending up consistently short then you probably like a little faster green. If you are always long, you probably prefer a slower green. The only thing important here is that you identify "your" speed. That is your "STANDARD".

Once you know: you know!

Now, take your standard to another golf course. Put the two quarters out again. Hit a couple putts. Make sure you keep your "STANDARD" speed in the stroke. If the ball is ending up short of the quarter, the green is slower. To adjust, the **last** thing you want to do is hit it harder. You only have to change where you aim. If you hit a putt and it ends up 12 feet instead of 15 feet, simply add 3 feet for every 15 feet you have on that particular speed of green. Or you can do the math. If the green is 20% slower, add 20% to the other side of the hole and let the speed of the green take care of the difference. For example, on a green that is 20% slower, if you hit the putt as if it were 18 feet, it will only go 15 feet. In other words, you NEVER have to change "your" stroke. You just have to know your STANDARD !!

A STIMPMETER is a device used by the USGA to measure the speed of greens. Basically, it is a flat, metal bar about 2 ½ feet long with a notch at the top that the ball sits in and a v-shaped channel the length of the bar. You set the bottom of the bar on the ground with the ball in the notch. Once you lift the notch end of the bar to a certain angle, the ball will exit the notch and roll down the channel. It builds up a precise amount of speed by the time it reaches the bottom of the bar. Once on the ground it will travel a precise distance depending upon how fast or slow the green is. The number of feet it rolls from the bottom of the bar will be anywhere from 7 feet on a really slow green to as much as 13 or 14 feet on extremely fast greens. 10 is considered to be about medium speed these days.

ONCE THE STIMPMETER reaches 20 degrees, the ball will leave the notch. This angle creates a ball that is traveling at a consistent speed at the bottom of the rail where it meets the green. However far the ball travels once on the green is the speed in feet.

CHAPTER 3

SAND

SITUATION

The more you understand sand, the easier it is to play from there. Many PGA Tour pros say that they would rather hit it in the sand than to hit it in the long grass around the greens. The reasoning behind that is that the sand is more consistent and predictable than the long grass. To understand sand, the first thing you have to know is that the controlling factor in sand is AIR. Not all sand cleaves together the same. Some sand is round and some is shaped more like a parallelogram. Depending upon the size and shape, sand may contain a lot of air, or only a little. For our purposes we will just call sand "fluffy", "medium", or "firm". You can tell a lot about the sand just by stepping in the bunker. The more sand you displace when you step in, the fluffier it is. The importance of knowing this is that the more air in the sand, the bigger the swing you have to take to get the ball to go the distance you want. Air

dissipates energy. As the energy being transferred to the ball is
reduced, the ball travels a shorter distance.

PROCESS

"Measure Up".

A great way to improve your sand game is to be organized.
I use the 4-part acronym

OBAS as a guide. If you can count to 4, (O=1, B=2, A=3, S=4)
you can play better out of the sand.

O is "open". Open the club 30 degrees or so in your hands,
not with your hands. It is important to distinguish the difference between the two. If you open the club with your hands
you will probably close the club during the downswing.
Having a too square club at impact will effectively minimize
the bounce on the club. And, the bounce is a very important
part of good sand play. It keeps the club from digging and also
creates a more consistent divot in the sand. If your divot is
smooth then your clubface is probably too square to the path.
If the divot is really rough, the bounce on the bottom of the
club is hitting the sand instead of the leading edge and that is
going to help bring the club, and the ball, back out of the sand.

B is "ball position". Place the ball on the forward side of
the stance about even with the armpit. The goal is to have the
club moving perfectly level to the sand at the point where the
club is under the ball. If the club is traveling steeply down, or
up under the ball, it is more difficult to control the depth of
the divot.

A is for "alignment". Align the body about six feet open to
the actual target. Swing, though, should be along the line of
the body, not at your intended target. If your divot is way

behind the ball, you are probably swinging inside out toward the target, instead of down the body line.

S is for "sand". The goal is to take a very consistent amount of sand all of the time. I place a quarter under the sand about ½ to ¾ 's of an inch below the ball. My goal is to remove all of the sand from the top of the quarter without moving it. That helps me in the setup to focus on the quarter instead of the ball.

If you follow OBAS as an acronym and execute the swing correctly, out of medium sand, a 30-yard swing on grass will produce a 10-yard shot from the sand. Out of fluffier sand you will have to take a 40-yard or so swing to hit it 10 yards and out of firm sand you might only have to take a 20-yard swing to produce a 10-yard shot from the sand. If this is not what is happening, check the depth of your divots and be sure that you are swinging along the line of the body.

CHAPTER 4

Chipping

Situation

There are only 3 rules in chipping: One: land the ball on the green. Two: land the ball on a level and smooth area when possible. Three: hit the ball as low as possible while satisfying the first two rules. Reasoning: You will always get a better first bounce landing the ball on the green. Plus, believe it or not, greens are not as good as they look. They have hard spots and soft spots. The lower the trajectory of the chip the more the ball will *skip* instead of react to the hard and soft spots. The skip is much more predictable. The *first bounce* is truly the key to consistent chipping.

If you notice that you are hitting what you think are good chips and they end up all over the place, watch that first bounce. Most likely it is a big part of the issue.

Process

"Measure Up".

Place a tee 3 feet off of the chipping green. Place another tee 3 feet on the green. We will assume that we are chipping to a "10", or medium speed green. Take out all of your clubs from the 6 iron to your lob wedge. Chip 5 balls with each club, starting with your 6 iron. The goal is to fly the ball from the tee off the green to the tee on the green, landing it as close as possible to that distance. Once you have chipped with all of those clubs, take a look at the green. If you are a good chipper, you will notice a group of balls that represents each club, the 6 iron group being the farthest away and the lob wedge being the closest. The groups should be about the same distance from each other, too. For you to create your STANDARD, you have to identify the carry/roll percentage.

My STANDARD carrying the ball 6 feet looks like this:

Club	Roll	Total	*Carry/Roll %
6	21	27	20/80
7	18	24	25/75
8	15	21	29/71
9	13	19	32/68
PW	10	16	38/62
GW	8	14	44/56
Lob	6	12	50/50

* THESE PERCENTAGES MAY BE FRACTIONALLY OFF. You can round them to 20, 25, 30% etc. to get a good feel for how they work.

It is not important that your percentages are the same as mine. What is important is that your percentages are consistent. Regardless of the trajectory of the 6 iron and the ratio it creates, the most important elements are ball contact and a consistent set-up. The set-up will only change on "specialty" shots. (Covered in my "Routine Success" book)

You might ask, "Why is this so important?" The answer is two-fold. One, it brings the target much closer to you. You just have to hit the ball to a spot. Two, it helps with club selection. And with a lower trajectory, you will have more control over that always important, *first bounce.*

CHAPTER 5

Trouble

Situation

The trouble with "trouble" shots is more in attitude than function. Much of the time, the focus becomes the obstacles in front of you instead of the shot itself. Mastering trouble is about focusing on the task at hand.

As you go through your decision-making process, visualize the shot that takes the obstacles out of play, starting with the one closest to you. If there is more than one, like a tree, a lake, a bunker, etc., work your way from closest to farthest away. Once you have decided on a shot, trust that the shot itself will take the obstacles out of play. Resist the urge to see the result of your shot before you have actually executed it. Also, as you decide on a plan of attack, ask yourself:

> *Have I practiced this shot?*
> *Do I have confidence in the shot?*
> *What are the odds of me being successful?*

Is the risk worth the reward?

Once that is done and you have chosen your shot, the obstacles are "gone", and you can simply execute the shot. If you are successful, pat yourself on the back, remember that exact situation in vivid detail, and know that you can use that success to help you in similar situations in the future.

PROCESS
"Measure Up".

To produce "trouble" solving shots, change your set-up as much as possible and your swing as little as possible.

The variables you are looking to change are:

Loft: move the ball forward to add loft, and to the back of your stance to hit it lower.

*If you are hitting the ball from medium to heavy rough, moving the ball forward might not be an option as it brings in more of the grass behind the ball.

Curvature: the clubface has to be closed to the path of the club to hit a hook and open to the path of the club for a slice. Keep in mind that closing the clubface tends to deloft the club and opening it adds loft.

The key issue when hitting "trouble" shots is eliminating the trouble from your mind's eye. By having a hugely diverse practice, where you practice shots from good and bad lies, sidehill, uphill and downhill lies and from dirt all the way up to deep rough, you will gain confidence and, more importantly, you will understand what you can, and cannot do. The more understanding and confidence you have in these types of shots the more you will make good decisions. If you are committed to the decision you have eliminated the obstacles.

If your focus remains on the tree, water, out of bounds, etc., you either don't have confidence in the shot you have chosen, or your head knows you should do something else.

----

*You should never hit a shot on the course or in competition unless you have practiced it and have confidence in it. Play the smart shot today and let that drive your practice for tomorrow.

CHAPTER 6

CONCLUSIONS

If you are a beginning golfer there is no doubt that you need to have good instruction, develop a method that works for you, and develop your skill. The benefit of including the Golf Standard is that it will help you identify the very best aspects of your game and allow you to improve at an accelerated rate.

To *"Measure Up"* simply means that you are taking stock of what you are doing, and using that in an effective way to play better golf.

My experience with conventional teaching is that it is limited to swing mechanics. That is all fine and good, but what if your instructor is just trying to teach you 'his' method? That method may not fit your physical ability or your understanding of cause and effect.

It makes more sense to have an understanding of what you are and are not capable of doing and making the very most of that. Your unique attributes need to be used to the fullest. These attributes include: strength level, flexibility, hand/eye coordination, time commitment to practice, understanding of the game, physical limitations, etc.

The amount of stability you have in your game or the level of improvement is within your control. With a little attention to detail and consistency you can get the results you are looking for. Utilizing the components of The Golf Standard you can take control of YOUR game.

The Golf Standard can hopefully give you guidelines. Where you go from there is up to you. Enjoy finding YOUR standard and enjoy this great game of golf!

PART II

ROUTINE SUCCESS

FOREWORD

Routines are an essential ingredient in golf. And while there are many ways to develop a good set of routines, I have put together what I think are the 5 "must-haves". Routines are one of the true cornerstones in golf. They keep things organized. They keep things simple. They help you to measure your results and progress. They can bridge the gap between practice, play and competition. They are reliable. Every successful PGA Tour player that I played with had them. Every good amateur had them, too. Whether you are trying to maintain or improve, they can be the key to your success.

Failing to Plan, is Planning to Fail
- Ben Franklin

My five routines are:
1. Practice
2. Tournament Warm-Up
3. Decision Making
4. Shot-Making
5. Post Shot Analysis

Study them, learn them, adjust them to fit your particular needs, and watch your golf game improve and evolve.

Jeff Mitchell
   PGA Tour Life Member
   PGA Life Member

CHAPTER 1

CHAPTER ONE

THE ROUTINE of a Good Routine

You might ask, "Why should I spend my time working on routines"? That is a good question. As human beings, we are influenced continuously by our surroundings. We are subject to peer pressure and we are slaves to what we see and observe. In golf, many times we will make choices that are not remotely related to our strengths because we feel like we "should" play a certain way based on conventional wisdom. If a good player would play a certain shot under a set of circumstances, then I should do the same? It only makes sense, right? Actually, it doesn't. Every golfer is different. Every golfer has a set of skills that enable them to play to their potential. Few golfers, though, are able to identify that set of skills that is unique to them and even fewer have figured out how to play to their potential. It is only by creating an organized, meaningful, consistent, and personal method of practicing and competing that you will realize what you are capable of. All of this is dependent upon your goals, aspirations and dedication. But, if you want to improve, learn, and compete, you owe it to yourself to set the groundwork. Get organized and you just might see a side of your game that you were not aware existed.

From beginner to professional, creating and being true to your routines, is the key to success and happiness in the great sport of golf. Defining your version of success and happiness is completely in your hands. Believe in yourself and believe in your routines. What you see in the following chapters is MY set of routines. Use them as a guideline to create your own. Ultimately, the best way to proceed is the way that works best for you and you alone.

CHAPTER 2

Routine #1 - Practice

- Are your practices structured?
- Do you have goals in mind?
- Can you measure your progress?
- When you play in tournaments, do you see yourself repeating old habits?
- Do you have a plan for YOUR future?

HERE ARE some guidelines to help answer these questions and streamline your practice:

- Write your intended practice down ahead of time. Otherwise, you will meander around and get far less accomplished. Value your time and streamline your efforts.

- Write down your long-term goals. They should extend out for at least two years.
- Keep an up-to-date record of your GIR %; Fairways hit %, up-and-down %, and putts per round.
- With your stats in mind, write down your short-term goals. These should extend no farther out than 3-4 months.
- Know your distances. From a sand-wedge to a driver, you need to know how far you hit the ball <u>in the air</u>.

- Challenge yourself in practice. See how effective you can be creating competition-like circumstances. Create consequences that have meaning, like no television or no dessert for a day. Practice like you play, or play like you practice. If you are serious on the course you need to be serious on the range.
- Break your practice sessions into goal-specific time frames. Ex: putting- 10 minutes, chipping-10 minutes, full swing- 30 minutes, competitive rehearsal-20 minutes, "playing the course"-20 minutes.

- Break your goal-specific time frames into pieces also. Ex: putting- 5 minutes on 3 footers and 5-minutes on speed control. Full swing- 10 minutes on wedges from 30 to 100 yards, 10 minutes on mechanical drills, 10 minutes on fairway woods and the driver. Keep all of it relevant to the stats you are keeping and your goals.
- Go through your last 5 tournament rounds and identify your 5 best shots in each round. Were the shot patterns similar? Did you hit those shots under similar circumstances? The goal is to find out where your strengths lie.
- Go through your last 5 tournament rounds and identify your 5 worst shots. Were they similar? Did you hit those shots under similar circumstances? The goal is to find out where your weaknesses lie.
- Practice to maintain your best shots. Practice your worst shots. Maintain your strengths while improving your weaknesses. Knowing your strengths and your weaknesses is key to making good decisions and driving your practice sessions on the range and on the course.
- Practice with specific holes on the course in mind. Specifically, holes that seem to give you trouble. Confidence can make a huge difference. Being successful on the range can translate to better results on the course.
- Update your stats in order to ensure that you are practicing with a purpose.

Time is a precious commodity.
Spend yours wisely.

CHAPTER 3

ROUTINE #2 - TOURNAMENT WARM-UP

Although called a "Tournament Warm-Up", this routine is important to every round of golf you play. It is no less important to be prepared for a casual round of golf with friends than it is the Club Championship, the US Amateur, or any other competitive round of golf. The next round of golf you play will have an influence, good or bad, on the round that follows it.

Being ready to play is key to your success. With a consistent routine comes consistent results. Confidence is an interesting and, often, fragile aspect of the game. Much of confidence is a subject of competence. A successful warm-up routine, that includes all of the elements of your planned strategy will help give you a sense of ease and confidence as you stand on the first tee. Be very aware of **YOUR** routine. It should be fluid and perfected as a part of your practice sessions. Take note of those parts that work well for you and those that don't.

The goal of properly executed Tournament Warm-up is that it puts you on your first hole ready to play. If you get there too early, you might "think" too much. Getting there late can cause anxiety, a two shot penalty or even disqualification. Timing in golf is huge. Your warm-up can set you up to play your best golf.

Hopefully, during the practice round you made out a good diagram of the greens. I have included an example of what I call a "green sheet". It shows accurate yardages including the depth of the greens, yardage to the top of plateaus or ridges, carry distances over bunkers, and a good indication of the slope at various points of the green. Before I start my tournament warm-up, I try to acquire a hole location sheet. I may or may not place the day's hole locations on the green sheet, but I review the hole location sheet with each green in mind, the weather that day, and with the strategy I have developed for each hole with that pin in mind. With a little practice, this entire process will take only a few minutes. It can have, though, a big effect on your tournament warm-up. You can insert competitive decision-making and shot selection into your practice. For example, the pin location on the 9th hole is very close to the left side of the green and behind a bunker. If you can reach that green in two, you can rehearse hitting a draw with a 3-wood or the club you anticipate having in that situation. If you can't hit the green in two, you will want to lay up on the right side of the fairway at a distance that gives you the ability to be aggressive to that pin. From the left side of the fairway, the bunker comes into play and shrinks the landing area of your approach shot.

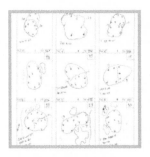

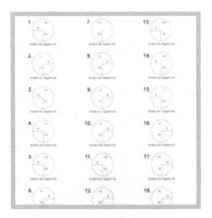

* This green sheet and the hole location sheet are not from the same course. This is for example purposes only. Both, though, are an integral part of your warm-up and success.

HERE IS an *example* of a structured tournament warm-up:

STRETCH in the locker room 10-15 minutes

PUTT 10 MINUTES

The putting green is the one place on the course that can

change the most overnight. Always start here in case you need to make a time adjustment. It is more important that you take the time you need than to feel uncomfortable on the greens on the course. I putt with one ball and make sure to go through the exact routine I use on the course.

CHIP 10 MINUTES

Pay attention to the first bounce. How the ball reacts could change depending upon how much water has been applied overnight or how the greens are mown. As you can see, I use a few balls and chip one ball to a variety of targets. I also chip from a variety of spots around the green.

Full swing 25 minutes
Have specific goals for your warm-up. It could include:

FULL SWING DEFINED

- Finding a good rhythm
- *Finding your rhythm might go like this: Start with a sand wedge. Use a basically full-length swing but only enough effort to hit the ball 50% of your normal full*

swing distance. As your muscles warm up and your feel improves, add effort gradually until you hit the ball as far as you can "under control". As you go through the bag (9, 7, 5, etc.), maintain the effort level you created with the sand wedge. If you get out of sync, go back to the sand wedge for a couple swings until you feel that rhythm again.

- Hit clubs you anticipate using during the round.
- Get a hole-location sheet when possible and rehearse shots with hole locations in mind.
- Rehearse the first couple and last couple holes you will play.
- Rehearse holes that you have not created a strategy for yet, or, that traditionally give you trouble. Make a decision about how you intend to play a particular hole prior to actually getting there.
- Finish your warm-up with a club you have a lot of confidence in or the club you will be using to start your round.

Variable time 5-10 minutes

FINISH WITH PRACTICE that is relatively close to your first hole when possible. You don't need any surprises right before you play.

Be sure to include time for a bathroom break if needed before you get to your first hole.

Be at your assigned hole 5-10 minutes prior to your official tee time. That amount of time should be comfortable for you and YOUR routine.

TOTAL TIME: 60-65 minutes

CHAPTER 4

Routine #3 - Decision Making

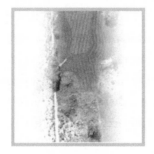

Decision Making - Before executing a shot, you must commit to your decision based on the facts of the situation.

These include, but are not limited to the following:

A. Lie - determines club selection and may limit options.

B. DISTANCE TO target - target is where the ball will land.

C. ALTITUDE- If your wedge goes 100 yards at sea level, it will go about 2-4 yards farther for every 1000 of elevation change, based on your club head speed. The faster you swing the club the bigger the distance difference.

D. ELEVATION TO target - a ball will travel approximately one yard shorter for every one yard uphill and one yard farther for each yard downhill.

E. WIND AND/OR other conditions - When playing into the wind, add 1 yard for every mph of wind up to 15 mph. Add 1 ½ yard for every mph after that. Crosswind is ½ yard per mph. These figures are for well-hit shots. They might not be exact, but they will give you a distance you can commit to. The wind will have a much greater effect on poorly hit shots.

F. TRAJECTORY and Curvature of shot - trajectory will add/subtract yardage and will affect roll, too.

G. BALL TYPE - Different balls allow you to create different amounts of spin. More spin keeps the ball in the air a little longer and will usually make it stop faster on greens. Less spin will give you more distance but a little less control on the ground. Ask your local pro about the balls you are using and why they might be a good fit to your game or not.

BEING ORGANIZED, consistent, and realistic about your decisions calms the brain and allows you to focus on the only thing that matters:

THE SHOT!

REMEMBER, you have 40 seconds to hit a shot once it is your turn to play. Know your strengths. Know your weaknesses. Commit to your decision.

For positive results, you have to control the ball **in the air and on the ground.** Have the information you need to make a good decision. A good set of notes, a detailed layout of the greens, and a well-made yardage book are great resources. Knowing what you want to do with the ball in the air is no less important than knowing what you want it to do when it strikes the ground. Be a control freak!!

DECISION-MAKING IS about confidence and commitment. A consistent mental routine creates a feeling of confidence, composure, and calm. It contains the following:

A. IMAGERY - REHEARSE seeing yourself performing the shot perfectly. Recall having been in this situation before and having had great results. From a "third-person" view, see yourself swinging the club. See yourself watching the ball in the air from contact with the club to the ball contacting the ground.

Watch as the ball comes to rest. The more vivid and detailed the image the better. You might even go so far as to feel the breeze, smell the air and grass, and notice the temperature. These images become your reality. You can choose what you see. Practice the process on the range and take it to the course.

B. PRACTICE SWINGS - Rehearse the shot physically with the actual shot vivid in your mind. If your "rehearsal" swing is successful, you need only repeat it. Your only limitation is time. You are required to play your shot within 40 seconds of when it is your turn to play. You can rehearse while others are playing their shots as long as you are not in their line of vision or disturbing play. Get into the habit of taking multiple rehearsal swings on the range when you practice. As you take rehearsal swings that are a great match to your decision, your confidence will grow.

C. FEEL – To execute a shot in your mind, you must be focused on the feel of the shot, instead of the mechanics or the outcome. When mentally engrossed in the shot, you eliminate fear, anticipation, obstacles (sand, water, spectators, etc.) and consequences. The shot takes over and the result takes care of itself.

ONE OF THE great things about decision-making is that you NEVER HAVE TO BE RIGHT, you just have to be COMMITTED! A committed swing will always be better than one that contains any level of doubt. Even if the result of the shot is not what you want, you will be able to identify the difference between what you wanted and what you got and improve your future decisions. An uncommitted swing will result in less than optimal shots a high percentage of the time. Plus, you will learn very little from a less than confident and committed swing that can help you in the future.

CHAPTER 5

Routine #4 - Shot-Making

Shot-Making - Once a decision is made, you should approach the ball the same as often as possible. From the time you begin to step into a set-up position for a shot a good shot-making routine will take the same amount of time on **all** shots. This will help you to treat all shots with the same importance level. Shots should not be thought of as difficult or easy. Your routine may vary from mine, but the elements should be similar.

Starting from about 6 feet behind the ball, my routine consists of:

GAP-T

1. **Grip** the club with the type of shot you have chosen in mind.

2. Take a stance and **Align** yourself with the beginning line of flight in mind.

3. Set up into a good dynamic **Posture**. This puts you in balance.

4. In your mind's eye revert back to the shot you have committed to and swing in **Tempo**.

FROM MY FIRST step toward the ball until I get to my finish position, my routine takes 11 seconds - EVERY shot, EVERY time. Learn to take the right amount of time for YOU. If it is too short, you will rush the shot. If you take too long, you will THINK your way out of the shot. With your mind focused solely on the shot your odds of executing the shot are drastically improved.

SEE IT, FEEL IT, TRUST IT!

CHAPTER 6

ROUTINE #5 - POST-SHOT ANALYSIS

POST-SHOT ANALYSIS ROUTINE - Once you finish your shot, take a moment to reflect. Ask yourself: Did I hit the shot the way I intended? If the answer is "yes" and the results were less than expected, try to figure out what ingredient you can alter in the decision making routine to correct it. If the answer is "no", I didn't hit it the way I wanted, rehearse the swing the way you intended. Either way, you are working on the direct result of the shot. Additionally, if you did not get the result you were looking for, the shot you decided on might have been what you "want" instead of what you are capable of. Choose a shot that is a strength in your game and gives you a high percentage opportunity for success.

Analyzing your shots **objectively** and making notes will drive your practice and help steer you toward more productive practice, better decision-making, and more overall confidence in your game. Being realistic in your shot choices, rather than being emotion driven, improves your odds of being successful.

For example: I have no idea what Jim Furyk is thinking after he hits a shot. My observations are that he is analyzing his execution of the shot he committed to as well as the result. He looks to be making mental notes of the decision he made and the result he got in comparison to the quality of the shot he actually hit. He is trying to figure out how to make a better decision in every circumstance. He also takes another swing or two before he leaves that spot. My observation is that he wants to leave every shot having taken the perfect swing. This is going to give him confidence the next time he has a similar situation.

Sometimes, even with the best of plans, the wind dies or the ball hits a hard spot. Try not to take it personally. You can improve your odds, but there are no guarantees. By staying objective and realistic you will be able to maintain your composure and learn for the future.

CHAPTER 7

THE VALUE OF ROUTINES

FOR THE VAST majority of people, golf is a difficult sport in which to be proficient. It has many facets, is played on an uneven and inconsistent surface, and it can be difficult to find clubs that are fitted correctly for your particular body style, strength level, etc. But if you are motivated to be as good as you can be or just want to be able to enjoy the game on a regular basis, your ability to be successful is wrapped around your knowledge and your organizational skills. Routines give you the ability to stay on the right path, to understand where you are in your game and why, and give you a road map for your future. Throughout all of my golfing life, I have been fortunate enough to understand the power of routines. It paid huge dividends for me and I am confident that it will for you.

Great Golfing!

PART III

GAME AND COURSE MANAGEMENT

FOREWORD

Golf can be a very complicated endeavor. It seems like every day is a new challenge and once you get one part of your game figured out, something else goes awry. If you recognize this pattern in your game, don't worry, you can make huge gains in your ability to manage your game and lower your scores.

Early on in my career, it dawned on me that for me to be successful, I had to identify patterns in my game that allowed me to get the most positive result possible from every shot. I found that it wasn't as important that I hit the perfect golf shot, but that I was paying attention to where I was leaving the ball. I played a lot of pool growing up. Being able to make the 4-ball in the corner pocket was great. But my success was ruled by where I left the cue ball. The same can be said in golf. Your distance from the target, in many cases, is not as important as the direction to the target and the degree of difficulty of the next shot.

One of the most important aspects of golf is the relationship between "Game Management" and "Course Management". Game management is the understanding you have of your own game. If you don't know your strengths, or how far you hit the ball in the air, or your general pattern of shot, it is difficult to create a functional strategy, which is course management. In fact, if you don't have a thorough understanding of what you do or how it is influenced by circumstances such as tournament pressure, course management is of very little practical use.

"Golf is 90% Mental...And the other 10% is Mental"
-Bruce Lietzke

Jeff Mitchell
  PGA Tour Life Member
  PGA Life Member

CHAPTER 1

GAME MANAGEMENT - FIRST THINGS FIRST

Before you start thinking about how you are going to approach a hole on the golf course, you should go through the process of identifying and understanding the parts of the game where you excel and the parts that you need to improve. Every golf course has strengths and weaknesses. It is up to you to play to your strengths against the golf courses weaknesses. The following is a roadmap to assist you along the way. After the form is a description that will help you understand each item. Your game will change over time. Some of the changes will be good and some will not. The more observant and objective you are about your game, the better you will implement a course management strategy that will give you better results. Be sure to come back to this information on a regular basis.

STRENGTHS AND WEAKNESSES

Strengths and Weaknesses
Rate from 1-5, 5 being best

	Date	Rating	Date	Rating	Date	Rating	Date	Rating
Short putt								
Long putt								
Sidehill putt								
Reading greens								
Low-lofted chips								
High-lofted chips								
Flop shots								
Pitch shots to 50 yards								
Pitch shots from 50-90 yards								
Short irons								
Long irons								
Fairway bunker shots								
Trouble shots: under trees, divots, restricted swings, etc.								
Fairway woods								
Driver								
Course management								
Shot selection								
Handling pressure								
Maintaining focus								
Routines: Practice								
Tournament warm-up								
Decision making								
Shot making								
Post-Shot Analysis								
Distance control								
Trajectory control								
Physical fitness								
Nutrition								

Short putt - percentage of putts made within 8 feet or so. Example: 3 feet and under – 90%, 4-6 feet – 60%, 6-8 feet – 40%.

LONG PUTT - PUTTS from 8-15 feet can be considered long. Any putts over 15 feet should be treated as a long putt. The realistic goal is to two-putt and go to the next hole.

SIDEHILL PUTT – Any putt that has to be played outside the hole. These putts require line and speed control. They tend to be the lowest percentage made.

READING greens – The difference between your read and result can be significant. The best way to improve is by experience and observation.

LOW-LOFTED CHIPS – The ball is within 6 feet of the edge of the green and the flag is 15 feet or more from the edge of the green.

HIGH-LOFTED CHIPS – When the ball has to carry more than 35-40% of the distance to the flag. Ex: the ball is 15 feet off the green and the flag is 15-30 feet on the green.

FLOP SHOTS – When the carry distance is more than 75% of the distance to the flag and the total distance is less than 30 yards.

PITCH SHOTS to 50 yards – A 'pitch' shot is a long chip shot with spin for control on the ground.

PITCH SHOTS from 50-90 yards – This is a big scoring area if you can control your launch angle and spin rate.

SHORT IRONS – PITCHING wedge up to a 7-iron

LONG IRONS – 6-IRON and up

FAIRWAY BUNKER SHOTS – Any fairway bunker removed from the area of the green by at least 25 yards or so.

TROUBLE SHOTS: under trees, divots, restricted swings, large curvature – Any shot that is a departure from a decent lie without obstacles in the way of the ball, stance, intended area of swing or flight of the ball.

FAIRWAY WOODS – When used off the tee and through the green.

DRIVER – CAN BE RATED by distance, accuracy and ability to control trajectory and curvature.

COURSE MANAGEMENT – Your ability to play to your strengths and to use post-shot analysis to influence future decisions.

SHOT SELECTION – ABILITY TO choose the correct shot for a particular situation.

HANDLING pressure – Your ability to eliminate interference (score, water, opponent, weather, etc.) and execute a shot.

MAINTAINING focus – Staying in the moment and maintaining objectivity.

ROUTINES: Staying vigil about the importance of and execution of a good warm-up, decision-making, shot-making, and post-shot analysis routine.

DISTANCE CONTROL – FULL SHOT AND 'IN-BETWEEN' club distance control

TRAJECTORY CONTROL – The ability to flight a ball higher or lower to gain control in the air and on the ground.

PHYSICAL FITNESS – The level of fitness needed to avoid fatigue during practice, play and competition.

NUTRITION – MAINTAINING a diet that promotes health and stamina. This can also include food and hydration that is ingested during practice, play and competition.

CHAPTER 2

IN THE AIR AND ON THE GROUND

Golf is both art and science. The art is the ability of a golfer to control a ball's trajectory, curvature, spin rate and overall distance in the air. Controlling the distance, trajectory, spin and the curvature of a shot is a subject of swing mechanics, experience, touch and feel. As you practice, pay attention to what the ball does in the air. Even if the shot you hit is not the one you intended, the accidental benefit is that you can get a "feel" for a wide variety of shots. The science aspect relates to what the ball does once it lands on the ground. The more you control the ball in the air and the more information you have about where the ball will land the more you can anticipate the result. *__Golf is not about perfection, it is about repetition.__* As much as your goal may be to have a swing like Adam Scott or Stacy Lewis, being able to "feel" a shot can be extremely useful. Bubba Watson has a very unorthodox swing. You cannot, though, argue with his results.

IN THE AIR

As you practice and as you play, pay careful attention to the effect trajectory and curvature have on your shots. Trajectory can influence how far the ball travels in the air. Low shots carry a shorter distance. A medium trajectory shot tends to give you the optimal carry distance. A higher shot will apex sooner and tend to fly slightly shorter. All of these statements change if there are weather conditions. Wind affects shots hit high and low. Temperature extremes have a considerable influence on the ball, too. The curvature of the ball can create different results, as well. A ball curving into a cross wind, in essence, turns it into a shot hit directly into the wind, thus the ball will travel a shorter distance. A ball traveling the same direction as the wind will travel farther. Figuring out how to create a trajectory and curvature that work under specific circumstances can be a huge advantage.

On the Ground

The reaction the ball has when it lands on the ground is dependent upon the angle of descent and the slope and condition of the ground it contacts. For example, if a ball is traveling right to left and the ground is sloped left to right, the ball will stop relatively quickly. If the ball and the slope are traveling the same direction, you will get much more distance out of the shot. Of course, this is also influenced by how hard or soft the ground is, too. To gain a lot of control of the ball, you have to ask yourself, *"Do I want the ball to go, or do I want the ball to stop?"* And, to be able to even ask this question you need to have the proper information that a yardage book, or GPS device or a really good set of notes can give you to anticipate the type of response you are looking for when your perfectly controlled shot in the air meets the ground.

"In the Air and On the Ground" is relevant in relation to your skill level. Regardless, though, of your skill level, you should always be striving to get the most you can possibly get out of your shots. You may think you are not good enough to get any gain out of information about yardage, slope, etc. If you think that way, you are correct.

As much as I love hitting great golf shots, the ability to score is where I get the most satisfaction out of the game. By taking advantage of my "art" ability and my "science" knowledge, I know I can.

CHAPTER 3

COURSE MANAGEMENT - IN A PERFECT WORLD

The type of strategy you employ to play the game of golf is not the most important part. It is only important that you have YOUR strategy and that it is in-line with your current ability level.

Whether you are an 18 handicap or scratch golfer, you need to formulate a strategy that allows you to maximize your results. Plus, your strategy should be fluid over time. The best way to do that is to continually analyze your performance by comparing the quality of the shots you hit with the results you actually achieve. Let's say that you have 175 yards to the pin and you choose a 5-iron. You hit the ball extremely well. It travels 180 yards in the air. It takes one bounce and goes over the green and you have a nearly impossible chip remaining. How is your attitude toward the shot? Are you mad, sad, or deflated? The problem is, you just hit a really good shot and ended up with a terrible result. It is likely that you will blame the wrong part of your game. It isn't the shot or the swing that is to blame; it is your decision.

If a PGA or LPGA Tour player had the same situation,

what would they have done? You may have noticed that the title of this chapter is "In a Perfect World". This might lead you to believe that the best players in the world aim at the hole all of the time. This could not be further from the truth. The best players in the world understand their own game enough so that they can get the "best" result possible. That might be 6 feet from the cup and directly below the hole, or it might be 45 feet from the hole and on the front of the green. Their choices are made based on the difficulty of the shot in front of them and their normal dispersion patterns. For even the very best of golfers, hitting a 4 iron within 10 feet of the flag a high percentage of the time is unrealistic. Depending upon your ability level, you have to give yourself a "target area" that allows you to be successful even if you don't hit your best shot. This may mean aiming at the middle of the green, or a little short, right or left of the green. By doing this, you can avoid trouble such as water, sand, or out of bounds and set you up for an easier next shot.

That being said, you should always look at ways to improve and get better results. By comparing your results to what the best player in the world would do can give you a benchmark. As you practice you can try shots that only the best would try and see how realistic that might be.

Always consider what you perceive as the "perfect" shot for the situation. Make decisions, though, based on your current ability level. You might see that by choosing the appropriate shot for you your confidence level goes up. Stay on the cutting edge of your ability and you will give yourself an opportunity to evolve as a golfer.

CHAPTER 4

COURSE MANAGEMENT - YOUR STANDARD

Every shot you hit should be based on your ability to actually execute that shot. If you were thorough with the "Game Management" form, you have probably noticed that you are really good at some things and not as good at others. This chapter is geared toward helping you identify a well planned out and effective approach to playing the game. The goal is to get the very most possible out of your game. By creating a STANDARD you can live by, you increase your chances of getting good results even from marginal golf shots.

How you play any given hole starts at the green. Based on how you rated different aspects of your putting you have to ask, "Where do I want to putt from?" To arrive at that spot on the green, you have to look at how you rated your approach shots. From there you go back to either the second shot on a par 5 or the tee shot on a par 4.

Example: #18 565 yards Par 5

HOLE DESCRIPTION: It is a relatively open tee shot. There is a creek in front of the green. The green has a lot of slope back to front. The pin is tucked behind a bunker on the right side of the green.

- **Strategy:** I would like to have a 10-foot putt from pin high left of the hole (it is on the fall line, and uphill).
- If I can reach the green easily, I can aim for the left side or center of the green. This is a logical decision if I am a good fairway wood player.
- If I cannot reach the green easily, and to be able to control my approach shot, I need to leave the ball at a distance where I have a great deal of confidence.
- For me that yardage is 80 yards. I can control the distance, trajectory and the spin and give myself a high percentage opportunity to have that 10-foot putt.
- For me to be able to reach the green in two, I need to hit my drive just left of center. This gives me a good angle to hit a second shot to the green.
- **Reasoning:** Statistics show that more putts are made and there are fewer 3-putts going uphill than there are going downhill or sidehill.
- A wedge at 80 yards is easier to control than a 40-yard

pitch over a bunker to a green that is level or sloping away from you.

- Giving yourself a little larger margin of error with the drive or second shot or a layup shot gives you more chance to make par. And if they are successful you will have more opportunities for birdie.

- This strategy works well with the strengths of my game. Regardless, your strategy should be formed in advance and have sound reasoning.

CHAPTER 5

ODDS ARE - MAKE THEM WORK FOR YOU

Much of golf is based on angles. Putts are influenced by up, down, and sidehill angles. Trajectory of shots influences roll as the ball strikes the ground. The angle of a green where the ball lands influences the way the ball rolls out. Elevated greens change the angle of descent of the ball on chips, pitches, and full shots. The ball generally comes in on a flatter trajectory to an elevated green causing more roll, and at a steeper angle when the green is below you allowing the ball to stop quicker. Your ability to place a ball in a particular area of the course is contingent upon creating angles and understanding how to make them work for you.

Your normal variances need to be considered also. If you hit 50 seven-iron shots, you will get a dispersion rate. Some shots will be 10 feet or less. Many shots might be between 10 and 30 feet away. And, there will probably be 25% or so that are more than 30 feet away. If this is true, you must use these "parameters" when making your decisions. If a pin is 15 feet from beyond a bunker, and you use that as your target, you will only get a small percentage of those shots close to the hole and the others will be difficult up-and-downs. But, on the other hand, if you aim 10-15 feet beyond the flag or to the side, your chances of getting the ball in an area where the next shot is easier, are much improved. By making these types of decisions you are taking trouble out of play.

Course Management and Game Management go hand-in-hand. The understanding of your own strengths and weaknesses, "game management", is key to proper decision-making and confidence. Strategy is also about making decisions. Remember that decisions must be based on that situation and that situation only. They must be based on fact and not emotion. They must be based on your capabilities. They can't be influenced by score, or where you stand in a match, or what you "want". You must be able to commit to your decision with confidence and trust. Fortunately, you NEVER have to be "right". You ALWAYS have to be committed. A confident swing will give you results you can learn from. A doubt filled swing will not. Your odds increase when you make decisions based on tangible information about the golf course and your shot-making ability.

When working on this strategy, many factors must be taken into account. When possible you want to putt from a level spot, or uphill in the 1/3 pie area. The green alignment rods in the diagram below represent the "fall" line (the middle rod) and the 1/3rd area that you would most like to putt from.

Even if the putt is a little longer, your ability to control the break will help you make more putts and eliminate 3-putts.

For chipping, it is easier to get good results if you have more green to work with than you do area (fairway, rough, etc.) to carry.

You can see in this illustration above, that the ability to get the ball close with the first ball is probably better than the second, or as you move farther away from the green. Approach shots are easier when you give yourself the needed amount of green to work with. When hitting tee shots and lay-up shots you should eliminate sand traps and severe undulations and mounding in between you and the hole, when possible. By doing so your margin of error is increased. Attempt to leave approach shots at a specific yardage if you can. For instance, a 75-yard shot into a par five is easier than a 30-yard shot if the pin is close to the front of the green or just over a bunker. A 25-30 yard shot can be easier than a 75-yard shot if you have plenty of green to work with. When deciding on your shot you must know the distance to the front, your target, any plateau on the green, carry distance over a bunker or mound and the back of the green. If you hit your best shot, you need to know that it will not go over the green. Know how far you hit your driver, fairway woods, and long irons so you can leave yourself with a specific distance, whether it is 150, 120, or even 175 yards. You must be able to take water hazards, trees, fairway bunkers, and doglegs out of play when you can, or at least minimize them. This is achieved by playing short of, past, left or right of those obstacles. As complicated as all of this information sounds, with a consistent decision making routine you will make decisions that are in line with your strengths. You will also gain confidence in knowing that you have made a good decision. With a little bit of practice your decision-making routine will only take a few seconds.

CHAPTER 6

TROUBLE SHOTS

When making strategic decisions, learn to eliminate obstacles nearest to you first. For instance: eliminating a tree just in front of you is more important than getting a 150 yard shot within 10 yards of the green. The water 20 yards from the green is of no consequence if you cannot get the ball over or around a tree first.

Work your strategy out from the ball. For example: you have a shot where you have to hit a ball under a tree, fade it, and hit it 165 yards to reach the green. But, the ball lies in grass in rough 4 inches thick. As much as you want to reach the green, you must deal with the lie first. The lie obviously limits your choices. The grass will not allow you to hit the ball low, because the ball will hit the grass after impact and go nowhere. Or, a variation on the same situation: you have a good, clean lie, you have to hit the ball under a tree, and fade it, but there is water in front of the green. It is not a percentage shot to think you can hit a ball 10 feet off the ground, carry water 150 yards away, and stop the ball on the green.

Remember, it wasn't a good shot that got you where you

are, so don't follow a bad shot with a bad decision. You must play shots that give you realistic chances for success, even if that success is 100 yards from the green or even hitting a shot laterally back to the fairway. A bad shot should only cost you one shot at the most. If you play to your strengths you might have a great opportunity to recover that shot.

CONCLUSIONS

Game Management and Course Management are equally important. By continually monitoring the strengths in your game and by using your powers of observation, you can learn to get more and more out of your game. There is a huge separation in the game between the ability to hit quality golf shots and the ability to shoot scores that represent that ability. Many of the answers are right in front of you. By improving your game management you are more and more able to employ better course management. As you practice and as you play, be objective about why you are successful and why you are not. This process allows you to play to your strengths and take advantage of golf course weaknesses. The goal is to be able to be as aggressive as is realistic in any circumstance. Learn YOUR game and take advantage of opportunities when they present themselves.

PART IV

TOURNAMENT PREPARATION

FOREWORD

As a 10-year veteran of the PGA Tour and the Champions
Tour, and after a 21-year career as a college coach at Texas
Tech, Stanford and North Texas, I have tried to impart the
importance of preparation for tournament golf on myself and
on all of the young men and women that I have coached and
taught. I relate tournament preparation to a final exam in any
subject you may have encountered in school or college. If you
study well you will test well. Practice should be rigorous.
Competitive golf should be fun.

Very early in my PGA Tour career, I was playing in the
Bing Crosby Clam Bake. It is now the AT&T Pebble Beach Pro-
Am. It was early morning on a Tuesday and I was about to
play a practice round at Pebble Beach. Pebble is one of the
most recognizable golf courses in the world. It has been called,
"The most beautiful meeting of land and sea in the world", by
some. I had not played it before. I was 10 minutes or so from
my tee time and was playing with Peter Jacobsen. Peter was
from Portland, went to the University of Oregon and had
played Pebble many times. I asked him before we left the
range how he played the 18th hole. It is a beautiful par-5 along

the Pacific Ocean with two iconic trees in the middle of the fairway at the landing area. Peter stepped just behind my right shoulder and waved his hand at eye level from left to right in front of me and said, "picture this". I will never forget that moment. He described the hole so well that it magically appeared on the range. Peter and I both hit a fade back then. Peter would tee his ball up on the left side of the tee box and aim about 5 yards to the right of the ocean and hit a hard fade. Trying to get the ball to land right at the base of the two trees. He said that if the ball landed below the canopy of the trees, it was a lot less likely to hit anything hard enough to get into any trouble. If you get the ball past those two trees you have a good shot at hitting the green in two. After practicing that tee shot 500 times and having played the 18th about 25 times, I don't recall ever missing that fairway. That moment on the range changed forever the way I look at preparing for a round of golf.

Jeff Mitchell
PGA Tour Life Member, PGA Life Member

CHAPTER 1

The "Home Course" Approach

SUCCESS IN TOURNAMENTS is influenced by a couple main factors: Your ability level and your preparation. It is important that you are aware of and understand what you are capable of doing, and more importantly, what you are not capable of doing. Golf is about improvement over time and you have to take a clinical look at where you are right now as you prepare for a tournament.

As you look to prepare for that upcoming event, be sure to make a list of the things that make you successful at your home course. Since most golfers play their best golf at home, the goal is to make every course your home course. The reasons you play well at home are the same ones you need to research in order to play another course well.

CHAPTER 2

BE REALISTIC

THE MENTAL SIDE of preparation requires that you be realistic about the way you play and have expectations that fit within that paradigm. For tournament golf, it is about being in the moment, or staying in the present. How you have played in the past or how you hope to play in the future is not relevant.

It is imperative that you prepare for the next tournament based on how you are playing right now. The goal is to play to your current strengths and exploit the weaknesses of the course you are playing based on a well-formed strategy.

Your "expectations" will have a great deal to do with how you handle adversity and, hopefully, great golf, too. Frustration is in direct proportion to expectation.

Back in my PGA Tour days, I remember hearing the guys always say, "Watch out for the sick guy." The reasoning behind that comment is that the sick guy's expectations were a little lower and so they didn't use emotion as a catalyst as much.

The distraction of not feeling well worked to their advantage. The bottom line is, it isn't about whether "things" will happen, because they will. It is about how you choose to deal with them.

CHAPTER 3

Questions That Need Answers

It is now time for you to get started with your preparation for a tournament. Once you enter a tournament, you need to gather as much information about the venue as possible.

The items that you need to know might include:

- The type of grass on the greens, fairways and the rough.
- The speed and/or anticipated speed of the greens.
- Availability of a really good yardage book.
- Hole location sheet from previous events at that course
- Any course set-up information- yardages, hole locations, shotgun or tee times, etc.
- Course characteristics such as forced carries, dogleg holes, long par-3's, elevation changes
- Distance to the course from the hotel, or wherever you are staying

- Location of restaurants if you aren't eating at the course
- General traffic patterns at the time of day you will be going to the course or to a restaurant before your round

---

TO GATHER this information you can call the golf shop. They are usually very helpful with information. You can also contact the tournament director if they are not working at the course where you are going to play. Past results and other valuable information can also be found on the internet and on apps that show yardages, flyovers, and pictures of holes on the course. Lastly, you might talk to friends that have played in the event in the past. They can be a very good resource.

CHAPTER 4

TOURNAMENT CHECKLIST

AFTER YOU HAVE GATHERED all of that valuable information, it is time to go through your checklist. By being well organized you can create a "Home Course" feel. This may be the most important part of your preparation. The more relaxed you are, the better you will play.

The following is an example of a tournament checklist:

TOURNAMENT CHECKLIST

Tournament: _____

Entry Deadline: _____ Application sent (date): _____
Completed on-line: _____ Confirmation: _____
Qualifying Date: _____ Site: _____
Practice round- Date: _____ Time: _____ Fee: _____
Caddy: _____ Fee: _____
Hotel: _____ Phone: _____
Confirmation #: _____ $_____ Room Type(s): _____
Depart: _____ Date: _____ Airline & #: _____
Arrival: _____ (Place & Time): _____
Car Rental: _____ $_____ Confirmation #: _____
Depart: _____ Date: _____ Airline & #: _____
Arrival: _____ (Place & Time): _____

IT IS a good idea to find a route or alternate routes to the golf course and print a map of directions from the hotel, or wherever you are staying, to the course. You should ask a tournament committee member or someone from the area about traffic patterns at that time of the year and with your tee times in mind. Check to see if food is provided on site and if it is going to satisfy your dietary needs. If the course does not have what you need, look for restaurants you are familiar with or that have been recommended and are in close proximity. The internet is a good source for that information, too. Many tournaments include information on meals and restaurants in their information packets. If you do not carry a laptop or smartphone with you, most hotels have a business center you can use for little or no money and you can even print out the results of your searches. Advanced planning can be a time and stress saver.

In advance of a tournament it is always a good idea to stay in a good routine. You should get plenty of rest, eat nutritiously, and drink a lot of water. All of these will influence your performance. Energy and focus can help you stay steady and confident.

Check the weather forecast for the days leading up to the event. Note any anticipated changes in temperature, wind speed and/or direction. Make notes of the direction holes travel in relation to North, South, East and West. Not only will this help you prepare for wind with each hole in mind, but the greens on holes that face South and West can become drier and firmer since they face the sun for a longer period of time during the day. The grass on these greens may be slightly different, and thicker, too.

Once you have completed your checklist, you can focus on the task at hand...playing golf.

CHAPTER 5

Practice Round Routine

IF YOU HAVE a practice round routine, great. With your checklist completed, you can put your plans into play. If you don't have a routine, create one!

Your routine should include cleaning and counting your clubs, making sure you have balls, gloves, tees, umbrella, permanent marker, ball marker, pencil, etc. You should factor in any time it takes to get to the practice facility and any time it takes to get to your first tee box.

It is important that you are able accomplish your goals and be ready to play at the appropriate time. If you are late to your tee or early, it can lead to anxiousness or nervousness. This can be significant even for a practice round.

Create and know the elements of your routine. By eliminating surprises, you can reduce your stress level and gather all of the information that you need for the tournament proper.

Note the wind direction during the practice round, but try

to hit shots with the anticipated weather in mind. If it isn't going to change from the practice round to the first round, that is great. If it does, though, you will be ready for it.

Be sure to compare the strengths and weaknesses in your game to the strengths and weaknesses of the course. If you happen to be a long hitter, you might be able to take advantage of the par 5's. If you have a strong short game, you can be more aggressive to hole locations that are close to the edge of a green.

As you go through your round, make note of the high and low areas of the course. Water goes downhill. The low areas are going to be softer and have thicker grasses. The same goes for the greens. Look for obvious high and low areas. This will influence how you read your putts and how the ball will react on the green. It may also influence the decision you make on your approach shots so that you can land the ball on areas that give you a little more control or an easier next shot.

Create a thorough diagram of the greens noting the "fall" lines. Putt on the greens with only one ball and go through the same routine you have for a competitive round. Make notes in your yardage book with slopes, grain, and anticipated hole locations in mind.

The biggest adjustment on most golf courses is the greens. Make your putting and short game practice a priority. As you formulate your strategy, these factors will guide you on where you can be aggressive and where to be aggressive to a more conservative target.

Below is an example of a diagram of greens with slopes and yardages to ridges, over bunkers, etc. included. This information can give you a much clearer picture of what you are trying to accomplish and confidence in your decisions.

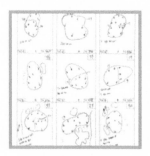

CHAPTER 6

Developing a Strategy

After accumulating as much information as you can find, spend goal-related time on elements of your game in practice that will allow you to maximize your ability level and potential. Also, spend time working on shots and situations that are rare, but important to your success. Examples would include hitting from bad lies, buried bunker shots, and lies with your ball in close proximity to a tree or overhanging limbs. You can also practice hitting shots after wetting your grips to prepare for rainy conditions. It is a good idea to don your rain gear to get comfortable wearing more clothes than normal. You can add a sweater or two to get the full effect if you are anticipating rough weather.

Once you complete the practice round, work on your strategy. Go to the practice facility and rehearse the shots you anticipate using on particular holes on the course. It will help you create confidence and help keep you in the moment. If you are preoccupied about how you are going to play the 15th hole, it might make it harder for you to concentrate on playing the hole you are on at the time to your ability. In other words, by preparing for the 15th hole in advance you can eliminate that as a distraction.

The night before the first round find a quiet somewhat dark spot where you can sit in a comfortable chair. Take some time to relax and clear your mind. Then, visually go through your upcoming round. Reconfirm the strategy you have create for the course with the anticipated weather, yardages, hole locations (if available) in mind. Always keep your strengths in mind and commit to your plan. Staying focused and confident will have a positive effect on your outcome.

CHAPTER 7

No Surprises

You don't need any surprises. OK, you have arrived at day one of the tournament. You have checked the weather, put your yardage book, clubs, balls, permanent marker, pencil, gloves, rain gear, umbrella, golf shoes, tees, band-aids, hand warmer, stocking cap, mittens and divot too in the bag or your car. Once you arrive at the course, you can put your tournament round routine into action. One added note: when you get to the course try to obtain a hole-location sheet as soon as it is available. (see below) Warming up with hole-locations in mind can be a big help. It could alter your strategy for certain holes and if there has been a change, you can avoid any anxiety or uncertainty that it might bring.

During the round, "use" other players in the group. Watch their shots, their chips and their putts. You know if they have hit it well or not. If they have similar shots, you can use that information to your benefit. The most obvious case is in putting. With your opponent putting on a similar line you are, in effect, getting the benefit of a practice putt. Position yourself, without being in the way, so that after they strike the putt you can easily move down their line and observe the speed and break of their putt.

Being in position and paying attention can give you a read on the speed and the line of your putt. That can be a big confidence booster for you in trusting your read.

CHAPTER 8

Be Observant

DURING YOUR ROUND, be observant. It is likely that this will not be the last time you play the course. You can gather information that will help you in tomorrow's round or the tournament the following year. You probably play your home course well. The more you know about a course, the more like your home course other courses will become. Use each shot, each hole and each round as an opportunity to learn for the future. It can help you in getting more out of the strengths of your game.

There are four stages of learning. The first stage is, "You don't know you don't know". If your superpower isn't observation, it should be. Otherwise you will never get past the first stage of learning. By being observant you can, "Know you don't know....Know you Know...and DO!!" It may sound a bit cliché, but it is critical to performance and success. Do you know where you are in the learning process?

CHAPTER 9

EVERY ROUND IS A PRACTICE ROUND

MAKE notes of the items that help you become successful in competitive rounds. Those might include your accuracy hitting fairways or your distance control. It might be that you have a strong short game. Make notes of things you may have missed in the preparation phase and practice round for this course. Keep statistics of fairways and greens hit, putts taken, and your percentage of up and downs. If you are even more thorough, there are any number of stats that can improve your future practice and your future competitions. Knowing that you had 32 putts may not be as important as looking at the difficulty of individual putts. Were a lot of your putts downhill or sidehill? The degree of difficulty on those putts is much higher. Or, if your up and down percentage is low it might be more of a reflection on your approach shots and where you are leaving the ball. If you "short side" yourself a lot your percentages might drop. A chip or pitch where you have little or no green to work with is a much more difficult shot. Angles can have a significant impact on results. This may seem that I have gotten a little off track, but continually paying attention to the little details, the strength of a course and your own strengths and weaknesses will help you get more out of what you currently have. It will also help you to plan your practice to strengthen areas that might not be as strong right now. The ability to save even one shot by being observant makes it worth staying engaged during the round.

———————

CHAPTER 10

POST-TOURNAMENT ANALYSIS

ONCE YOU HAVE COMPLETED the tournament, assess your results. Did you do all that you could have done to prepare? Were you able to take notes on areas that you may have overlooked in the preparation phase? Rate yourself on: staying in the moment, staying consistent to your strategy, playing to your strengths, adjusting to the changes in the course, adjusting to the weather, and maintain your composure. This information can make you a better player in the future. The goal is to maximize your potential by taking an objective look at your results and your patterns. The more you recognize, the better you will prepare for the next tournament. Your past will only dictate your future if you learn from it.

CHAPTER 11

CONCLUSIONS

THE REAL QUESTIONS ARE:

- Were you successful?
- Did you prepare as well as you could have?
- What would you do differently or better if you had it to do again?

AS YOUR EXPERIENCE grows and as your golf game evolves, one of the great benefits of proper tournament preparation is that you will see yourself getting more out of whatever level of golf you happen to be playing right now. You will see that you have fewer and fewer limitations. You will utilize your time better and you will enjoy the game more.

The benefit of doing your homework before you compete

is that it will carry over into the way you practice. It will build confidence in your decision-making and it will alter the way you look at your results.

Take ownership of your game and reap the benefits!!

ABOUT THE AUTHOR

Jeff Mitchell is an emerging author and professional golfer. He has played golf throughout the world including the PGA Tour and Champion's Tour.

The Golf Standard is his way of giving advice gleaned from his ten years of PGA Tour/Champions Tour experience, 30 years of teaching, and 21 years of coaching while sharing his love of the game.

You can stay in touch with Jeff here...
https://www.facebook.com/JeffMitchellGolf
https://www.twitter.com/jeffkmitch

www.golfswing.com